Contents

Any words appearing in the text in bold, **like this**, are explained in the Glossary.

Making colours

How many different colours do you think there are? Our eyes can see thousands of colours, some bright, some of them dark. Red, yellow, and blue are called **primary colours**. They cannot be made by mixing together other colours. Primary colours can be mixed to make every other colour.

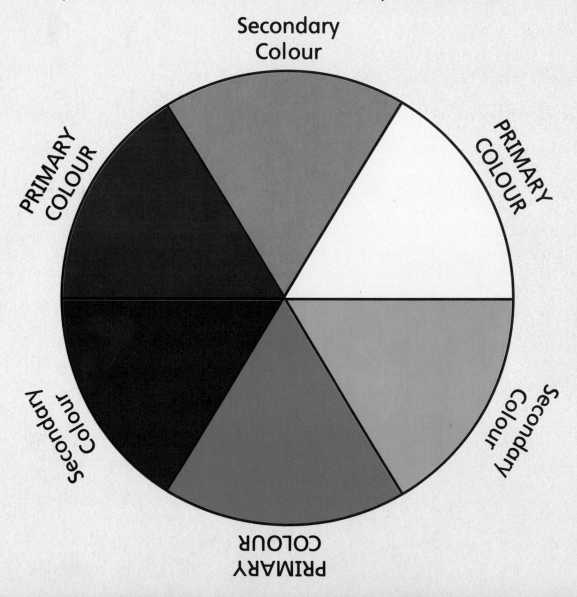

Secondary Colour

PRIMARY COLOUR

Secondary Colour

PRIMARY COLOUR

Secondary Colour

PRIMARY COLOUR

How Artists Use
Colour

REVISED AND UPDATED

PAUL FLUX

Heinemann
LIBRARY

H **www.heinemann.co.uk/library**
Visit our website to find out more information about Heinemann Library books.

To order:
☎ Phone 44 (0) 1865 888066
🖹 Send a fax to 44 (0) 1865 314091
💻 Visit the Heinemann Bookshop at www.heinemann.co.uk/library to browse our
catalogue and order online.

First published in Great Britain by Heinemann Library,
Halley Court, Jordan Hill, Oxford OX2 8EJ, part
of Harcourt Education. Heinemann is a registered
trademark of Harcourt Education Ltd.

Editorial: Clare Lewis
Design: Joanna Hinton-Malivoire
Picture research: Melissa Allison
Illustrations by Jo Brooker/Ann Miller
Production: Julie Carter

Printed and bound in China by South
China Printing Co. Ltd.

13-digit ISBN 978 0 431 16212 6
11 10 09 08 07
10 9 8 7 6 5 4 3 2 1

British Library Cataloguing in Publication Data
Flux, Paul
How Artists Use: Colour.
701.8'5

Acknowledgements
The publishers would like to thank the following for
permission to reproduce photographs:
AKG, London: pp. **7**, **9**, **14**, **17**, Munch Museum,
© Munch Museum/Munch - Ellingsen Group, BONO,
Oslo/DACS, London 2006 p. **19**, © ADAGP, Paris and
DACS, London 2001 p. **27**; Bridgeman Art Library:
© Kate Rothko Prizel & Christopher Rothko ARS, NY and
DACS, London 2006 p. **12**, © Succession Miro/ADAGP,
Paris and DACS, London 2006 p. **18**, National Gallery
of Scotland, Edinburgh / © ADAGP, Paris and DACS,
London 2001 p. **16**, Peter Willi p. **11**; Trevor Clifford
/ Jo Booker: pp. **23**, **24**, **25**; Corbis: National Gallery,
London p. **28**; The Museum of Modern Art, New York
/ © 2001 Mondrian/Holtzman Trust c/o Beeldrecht,
Amsterdam, Holland & DACS, London p. **20**; Bookmalli
Aboriginal Artists. Purchased with the assistance of
funds from National Gallery admission charges and
commissioned in 1987. Collection; National Gallery
of Australia, Canberra / DACS, London 2006: p. **15**;
SCALA: p. **10**; Tate, London 2006/Courtesy of Howard
Hodgkin: p. **13**.
Cover photograph of *Trees by a Lake, Le Parc de Carrieres
- St Denis*, 1909, reproduced with permission of ©
ADAGP, Paris and DACS, London 2006; Photo: Corbis/©
Albright-Knox Art Gallery.

Every effort has been made to contact copyright holders
of any material reproduced in this book. Any omissions
will be rectified in subsequent printings if notice is given
to the publishers.

Secondary colours are made by mixing two primary colours together. By adding more of one colour you get different **shades**. If you mix all three primary colours together you get a muddy brown! Not all animals' eyes work in the same way as ours. Many see a world in which everything is colourless.

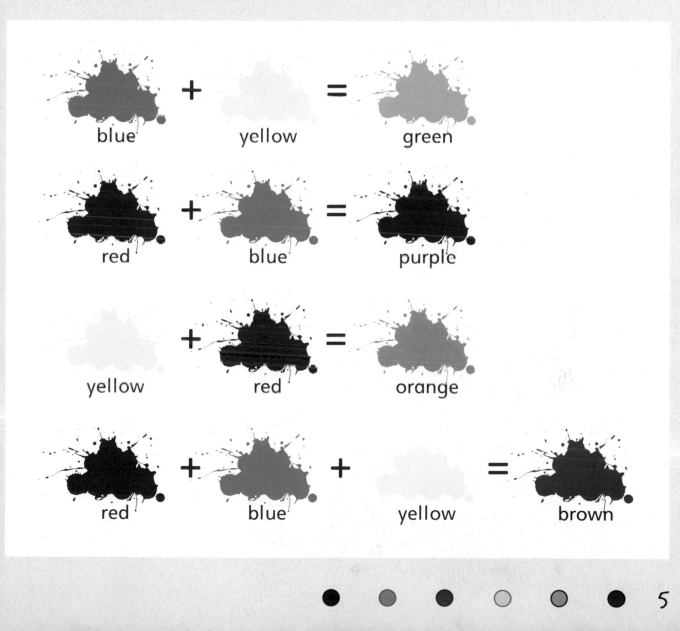

blue + yellow = green

red + blue = purple

yellow + red = orange

red + blue + yellow = brown

Colour partners

Opposite colours on the colour wheel (see page 4) **complement** one another. This means that they work together so that they both stand out. Which red blob seems strongest to you? All three are exactly the same, but the one on the green background seems much brighter. Can you see how the purple and orange blobs both seem very bright because they are with their **complementary colours**?

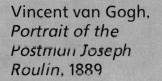

Vincent van Gogh,
*Portrait of the
Postman Joseph
Roulin*, 1889

Van Gogh is well known for his use of complementary colours.
The orange of the buttons and the postman's beard are used
as complementary colours against the blue coat. The green
eyes are strong and searching. Look at him for a while. Is he
looking at you, or past you? What do you think is on his mind?

Warm and cool colours

Warm colours remind us of fire and sunshine. They are red, yellow, and orange. Often artists use these colours to show strong feelings. The cool colours are blue and green. These make us think of the sky and the sea. When artists use cool colours their pictures can seem cold and lacking in feeling.

The French artist Paul Cézanne used warm colours to give his pictures great strength. Here he has placed fruit on a white cloth and surrounded it with **earth colours**. The warm colours bring the **scene** to life. They make the ordinary objects seem extra special. Have you ever seen apples look so dazzling?

Paul Cézanne, *Apples and Oranges*, 1895–1900

Colour makes a difference!

Colour can add meaning to many types of art. Look at these ancient Egyptian letters, which we call **hieroglyphs**. The walls of the tombs of kings were often covered with religious writing like this. The colours do not change any of the meaning, but the yellows, greens, and browns make the writing more **decorative**. Can you make your own writing more interesting by using different colours?

Egyptian hieroglyphic writing

Rose window, Notre Dame Cathedral, Paris, about 1250

Stained glass is found in churches and has been used for hundreds of years. This window was made more than 700 years ago. Light floods through the glass and fills the inside of the church with bright colours. People standing beneath this window can be covered with rainbow colours, which change as the light outside changes.

How artists use colour

Artists use colour in many ways. This painting is by an artist called Mark Rothko. He used big blocks of colour with fuzzy edges to show different moods and feelings. This kind of art is called **abstract**. It uses colour and shape to create mood rather than showing something realistic. How does this painting make you feel?

Mark Rothko,
White Cloud Over Purple, 1957

Howard Hodgkin, *Dinner at West Hill*, 1964–66

Howard Hodgkin painted this picture. It celebrates a party
held by a friend of his. Hodgkin painted the scene from
memory. The blocks of colour show how the artist remembers
the decoration of the room and the atmosphere of the event.
The horizontal line through the middle is the dining table. Do
you think the artist enjoyed the party?

Colour adds meaning

This painting is on the wall of a **monastery** in Florence, in Italy. The angel Gabriel is kneeling in front of Mary to tell her that she will give birth to Jesus, the Son of God. Look closely at Gabriel's wings. The blue and orange feathers **complement** one other, and so do the red clothes and green grass. The gold colour of the halos showed that the people were special.

Fra Angelico, *The Annunciation*, 1437–45

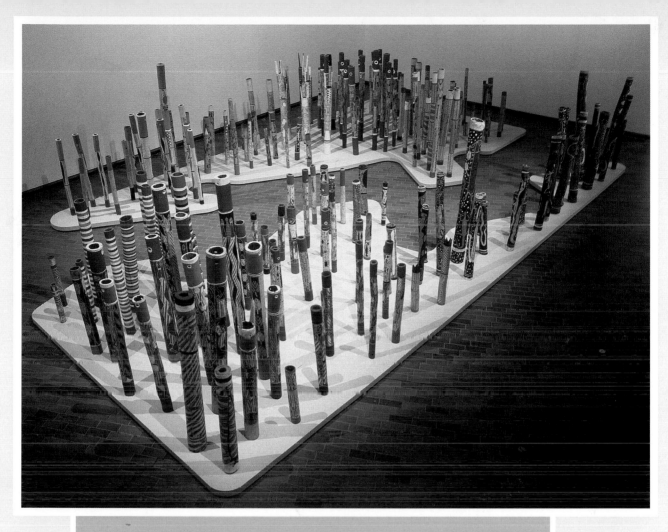

Ramingining Artists, *The Aboriginal Memorial*, 1987–88

Around 200 years ago, people from Europe discovered Australia and moved there. In 1988 many Australians celebrated this event. The **Aboriginal** people had mixed feelings because settlers had taken much of their land. A group of 43 artists made this forest of hollow log bone-coffins, some over 3 metres (9 feet) tall. The natural **earth colours** and ancient **designs** celebrate the Aboriginal culture.

Colours in balance

The French artist Claude Monet was interested in the effect of light on everyday **scenes**. He painted many pictures of the same places at different times of the day. In this beautiful painting he has balanced the blue light of early evening in winter, with an orange sky. Can you sense the stillness? The colours **combine** to create a feeling of great peace.

Claude Monet, *Haystacks: Snow Effect*, 1891

Caspar David Friedrich, *The Monk by the Sea*, 1808–10

Many paintings work well when the colours are used in balance. Here we can see a cloudy sky reflected onto a bare cliff top. The blue **tones** weave together to create a feeling of enormous space. The lone man gazing into the distance seems so small, set against the huge sky. What would you think about if you were standing there?

Colours that shout!

Colours can be used in ways which surprise us. In this picture, dark night-time shapes are surrounded by strong splashes of colour which seem to leap off the **canvas**. But these bright **tones** are held in check by a mysterious darkness. Think about the title of the painting. Would you want to be alone on a night like this?

Joan Miró, *Figures in the Night*, 1960

18

Edvard Munch,
The Scream, 1893

Bold colours are used again here, to give the painting its
strength. Swirling **shades** of red and orange push out from
the canvas. Is the figure a man or a woman? Notice how
the bright colours add to the excitement of the painting.
Do you think the scream is one of terror, or excitement?

Colour and the modern world

This was one of Piet Mondrian's last paintings. All his life he experimented with **primary colours**. He painted **abstract** pictures using yellow, red, and blue. He also used grey and white blocks, and black lines to separate them. The straight lines of New York city's streets gave Mondrian the idea for this painting.

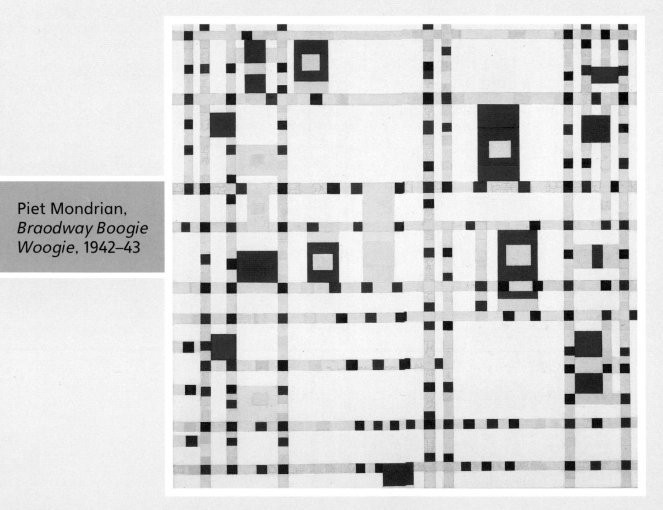

Piet Mondrian, *Braodway Boogie Woogie*, 1942–43

Today we can use computers to make great pictures. Colours, lines, and shapes can all be changed very quickly and you can repeat patterns easily. If you have a good printer the results can be very exciting. You can even use the computer to send your picture to a friend in another country!

Mixing colours

Mixing colours means you can create lots of different **tones** and **shades** to produce great artwork.

Do it yourself!

1. Start by painting a circle of one of the **primary colours**.
2. **Experiment** by adding different colours to it.
3. Keep a record of which colours you have mixed and the new colours you make.
4. Use the different shades you have made to paint something simple such as the sky, water, or a field of grass.

Do it yourself!

1. Collect lots of coloured see-through sweet wrappers.
2. Tape some of the wrappers to a window and **overlap** them to make different colours.
3. Make as many different colours as you can. If you want to make a colour stronger, fold the wrapper in half.

Colours working together

When colours move, our eyes can see things which are not there.

Do it yourself!

1. Cut out a circle of cardboard 15 cm (6 inches) wide. Ask an adult to make two holes about 1 cm (½ inch) from the centre.
2. Draw a design on one side and colour it. Repeat the design on the other side, but colour it differently.

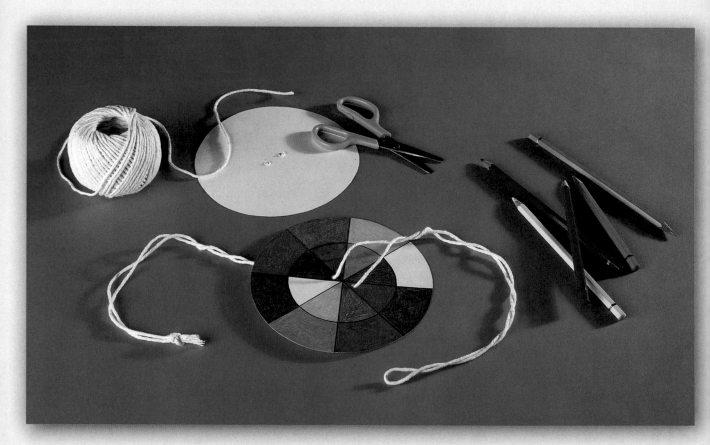

3. Get some thin string or yarn and thread it through the two holes. Knot the string to make a loop.

4. Hold the string in both hands. Twist it, then gently pull. As the card spins you will see the colours change.

5. Think about the way the colours work together. Which **combinations** of colour work best? What happens when you only use two **primary colours**? What happens to spinners that are just black and white?

Colours and tones

Tone ladders like these can help you find **shades** that go well together.

Do it yourself!

1. Put two big blobs of a **primary colour** paint on a **palette**.
2. Slowly add white paint to one of the blobs.
3. Add tiny amounts of the **complementary colour** to the other blob.
4. As you discover different shades, make your own tone ladders like the ones below. Tones that line up with each other on the ladders often work best together.

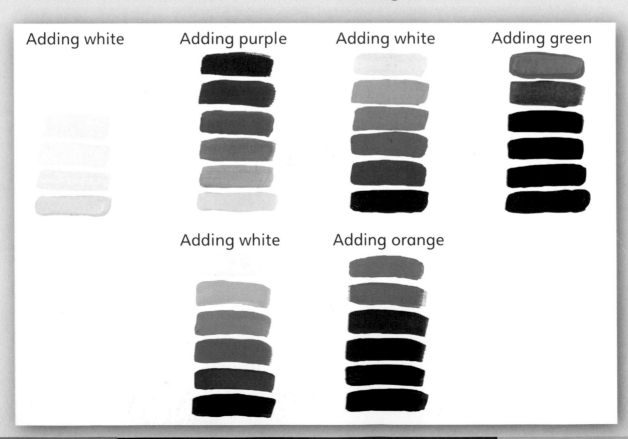

Adding white   Adding purple   Adding white   Adding green

Adding white   Adding orange

Here Claude Monet has used the light and dark tones of purple, blue, and green to paint his lily pond. The delicate colouring suggests that the time is early morning or evening. Monet was interested in the way the light and water **interacted** to keep changing the scene. He eventually painted his lily pond many times, and each picture is different.

Claude Monet, *Waterlilies*, 1907

Painting with dots and dashes

Georges Seurat was an artist who **experimented** with colour in a **scientific** way. He did not paint with **brush strokes**, but used tiny dots or dashes of colour instead. Look at the boy to the right of the picture. He seems surrounded with bright light. Seurat used light and dark **tones** and mixed them together to create this special effect.

Georges Pierre Seurat, *Bathers at Asniéres*, 1883–84

This way of painting tricks us into seeing many colours. The colours do not blend together on the **canvas**, but in our minds we see the blended colours.

Do it yourself!

1. Make a simple picture using only dots of colour.
2. Experiment using different shades of the same colour rather than blending them together.
3. Try combining different colour dots in the same area. What effect does it make?

Glossary

Aboriginal native person of Australia

abstract kind of art which does not try to show people or things, but instead uses shape and colour to make the picture

brush strokes marks in paint made by a brush

canvas strong woven material on which many artists paint

combination two or more things together

complement to make another colour seem bright

complementary colour a colour opposite another on the colour wheel

decorative pleasant or interesting to look at

design lines and shapes which decorate art

earth colour warm colour found in nature, such as brown or red

experiment to try things out, or repeat something until you like the result

hieroglyph symbol used by the ancient Egyptians in picture writing

interact how things work with each other

monastery building where monks live and pray

overlap partly cover

palette board used to mix colours on

primary colour red, blue, and yellow – colours that cannot be made by mixing other colours

secondary colour a colour which is made by mixing two primary colours together

scene view painted by an artist

scientific like science, testing ideas in an ordered way

shade a darker or lighter version of a colour

stained glass small pieces of coloured glass put together to make a picture

tone shades and depth of colour, from light to dark or dull to bright

More books to read

Connolly, Sean. *The Life and Work of: Claude Monet*. Oxford: Heinemann Library, 2006.

Connolly, Sean. *The Life and Work of: Vincent van Gogh*. Oxford: Heinemann Library, 2006.

Thomas, Isabel. *Action Art: Using Colour*. Oxford: Raintree, 2005

Index

Titles in the *How Artists Use* series include:

Hardback 978-0-431-16212-6

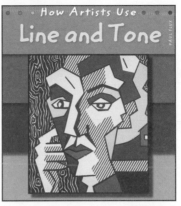

Hardback 978-0-431-16213-3

Hardback 978-0-431-16214-0

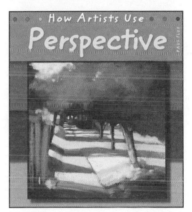

Hardback 978-0-431-16215-7

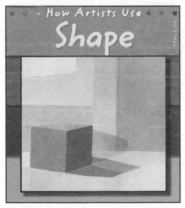

Hardback 978-0-431-16216-4

Find out about other titles from Heinemann Library on our website www.heinemann.co.uk/library